What Makes You Cough, Sneeze, Burp, Hiccup, Blink, Yawn, Sweat, *and* Shiver?

Jean Stangl

My Health

Franklin Watts

A Division of Scholastic Inc.

New York • Toronto • London • Auckland • Sydney

Mexico City • New Delhi • Hong Kong

Danbury, Connecticut

For Ken

Photographs©: Corbis-Bettmann: 35 (Roger Ressmeyer); Custom Medical Stock Photo: 40 (Richard Wehr), 13; Laura Dwight: 11; Medichrome/StockShop: 10 (Friend & Denny), 39 (Harry J. Pizekop, Jr.), 9 (Tom Raymond); New England Stock Photo: 29 (Eric R. Berndt); Peter Arnold Inc.: 12 (Matt Meadows); Photo Researchers: 38 (David Gifford/SPL), 22 (Carlyn Iverson), 8 (Saturn Stills/SPL); PhotoEdit: 6, 24 (Mary Kate Denny), 26 (R. Hutchings), 20 (Felicia Martinez), 4, 34 (David Young-Wolff); The Image Works: 36 (B. Daemmrich), 37 (Townsend P. Dickinson), 32 (John Eastcott/Yva Momatiuk), 15 (Jeff Greenberg), 27 (Boyd Norton); Tony Stone Images: 23 (Ian Shaw); Visuals Unlimited: 31 (Kjell B. Sandved).

Cartoons by Rick Stromoski, illustrations by Pat Rasch and Leonard Morgan

Library of Congress Cataloging-in-Publication Data

Stangl, Jean.

What makes you cough, sneeze, burp, hiccup, yawn, blink, sweat, and shiver? / by Jean Stangl.

p. cm.—(My Health)

Includes bibliographical references and index.

Summary: Describes what makes people cough, sneeze, burp, hiccup, yawn, and have other such reflex responses and explains the role these actions play in maintaining health.

ISBN 0-531-20382-4 (lib. bdg.) 0-531-16510-8 (pbk.)

1. Reflexes—Juvenile literature. 2. Belching—Juvenile literature. 3. Hiccup—Juvenile literature. [1. Reflexes.] I. Titles II. Series.

QP372.S82 2000

612.8—dc21 99-049741

Printed in China.

19 20 21 22 R 15 14 13 62

Contents

Out of Your Control

Cough! Cough! Something is tickling your throat. It could be a piece of dust that you happened to breathe in, or maybe a little **mucus** is dripping down your throat from your stuffy nose. If you were eating too fast, a piece of food may have slipped down your **trachea** instead of your **esophagus**. Coughing is your body's way of clearing your throat so that plenty of air can get to your lungs.

Aaaaah CHOO! You don't mean to sneeze in the middle of class, but you can't help it. You don't tell your body to sneeze, it just happens. A sneeze is your body's way of clearing particles from your nose so that you can breathe better.

Did You Know...

Just one sneeze may spray as many as 100,000 drops of mucus and germs into the air. If you have a cold, cover your mouth when you sneeze. You do not want people around you to breathe in your germs.

◀ **This boy is coughing because he has a cold. He is about to cover his mouth so he won't spread germs.**

You can't control when you sneeze. Sometimes it happens so fast that you don't even have time to cover your mouth.

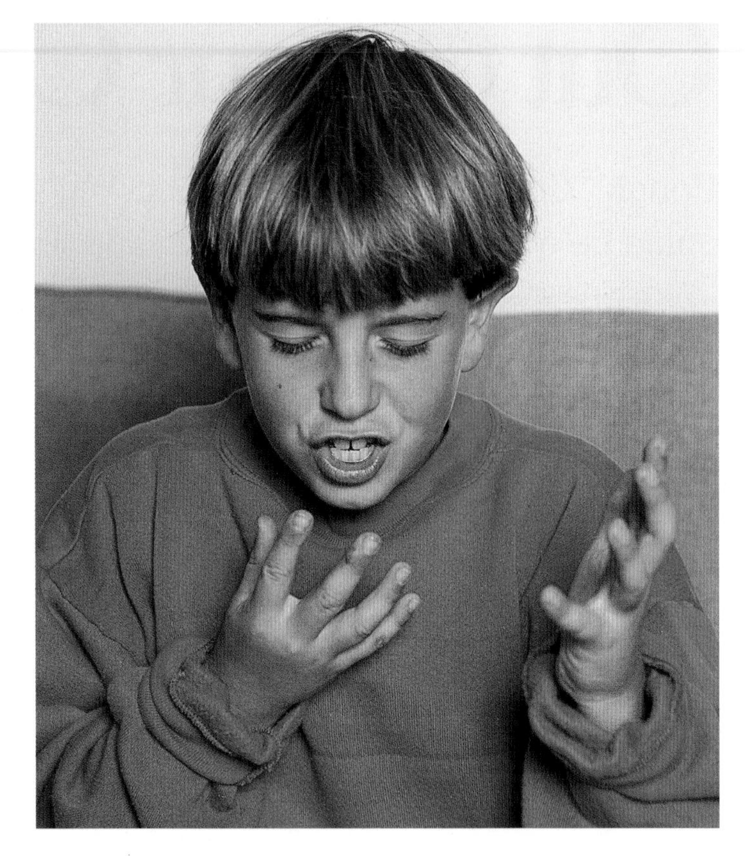

You can control when you walk and when you talk, but you can't control when you cough or sneeze. Your brain can make your body do many things without you even thinking about it. These body actions are called **involuntary reflex actions.** Coughing and sneezing are involuntary reflex actions, and so are burping, hiccuping, yawning, blinking, sweating, and shivering. To learn more about what causes these actions and how they help keep you healthy, read on.

What Makes You Cough and Sneeze?

When you cough a lot, the **mucous membranes** in your mouth and throat dry out. So if you are doing a lot of coughing, you need to drink more water than usual. Cough drops and cough syrup may also help. They reduce coughing by temporarily blocking your cough reflex.

Throat Frogs

Have you ever heard someone say, "I have a 'frog' in my throat"? Of course, this is just an expression. It means that something—mucus, dust, or some other material—is stuck in the person's throat. When the person tries to talk, his or her voice sounds like a croaking frog. You can get rid of a frog in your throat by coughing or clearing your throat.

What Is Whooping Cough?

Whooping cough is a highly **contagious** children's disease that causes a fever and a dry cough. A dry cough means you can't cough up any mucus. The coughing comes in spells and often causes vomiting. Coughing attacks may occur several times a day, and may last up to 5 weeks. Because most children in North America are **vaccinated** against whooping cough when they are very young, you probably do not know anyone who has had this disease. You can check your health records to find out if and when you were vaccinated against whooping cough.

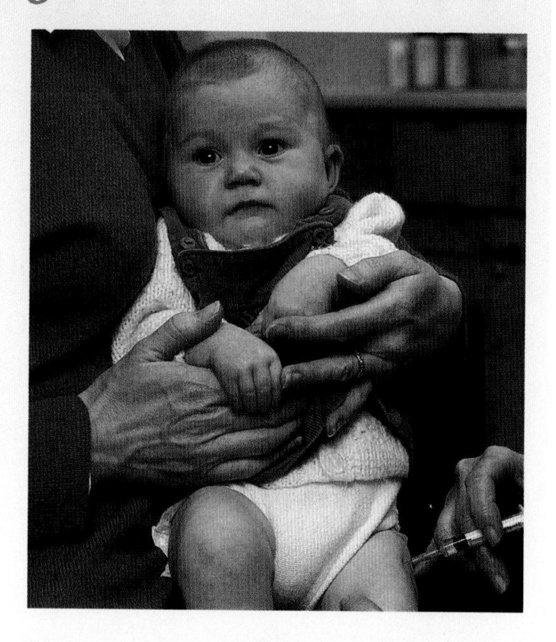

You were probably vaccinated against whooping cough at about the same age as this baby.

Have you ever made yourself cough because you wanted to clear your throat? When you make yourself cough on purpose, it is not an involuntary reflex action. You are controlling the cough, so it is a **voluntary muscle action**.

This girl is coughing voluntarily because ▶ she wants to clear her throat.

This woman is adding pepper to a chicken. If she breathes in too much pepper, she may sneeze.

It is not so easy to make yourself sneeze. Looking toward the sun or a bright light makes some people sneeze. ***Do not look directly at the sun, it could hurt your eyes***. You may also be able to make yourself sneeze by breathing in pepper.

When the tiny pepper particles land on the hairs inside your nose, **nerve endings** in your nose sense that you have breathed in something that doesn't belong there. They send a message to your brain. Less than a second later, your brain sends a message to other nerves in your lungs and—aaaaah CHOO! Your lungs send up a burst of air that blasts out the unwanted visitors.

Some people say they can make themselves sneeze by scratching lightly between their eyebrows. This may be because the nerves there are closely connected with the nerves in your nose. When you scratch that area of skin, you irritate the nerves in your nose. Your brain thinks that there are particles in your nose and makes your body sneeze.

The Polite Thing to Do

How many times have you heard, "Don't sneeze on me!" or "Cover your mouth when you cough!"? Covering your mouth when you sneeze or cough is supposed to be good manners. After all, you don't want to send your germs out into the air that other people are breathing. But coughing into your hand leaves germs there—germs that may spread to somebody else through touching. So should you cover or not cover? The best answer: Cover your mouth and then wash your hands! Or cough or sneeze into a tissue and throw it away immediately.

You should wash your hands with soap and water after coughing or sneezing.

When you sneeze, air, moisture, and germs blast out of your mouth and nose.

Put your hand in front of your nose the next time you start to sneeze, and you will feel a blast of air. Scientists have measured the speed of air rushing out during a sneeze at more than 100 miles (160 km) an hour.

If you want to keep yourself from sneezing, try this trick the next time you feel a sneeze coming on: Place your finger under your nose and press hard. By putting pressure on the nerves under your nose, you may be able to stop the sneeze.

This boy is trying to stop a sneeze. Do you think he'll be successful?

Activity 1: How Many Sneezes?

When you sneeze, do you usually sneeze just once or does it take two or three sneezes to clear out your nose? Do you ever sneeze more than three times in a row? Keep track of your sneeze patterns and write down what you notice in a notebook. Ask a few friends to do the same thing and compare your results.

You may also be able to stop a sneeze by closing your mouth when the sneeze starts, but this is not easy. The same involuntary reflex that makes air blast out of your nose and mouth also causes your mouth to fly open and your eyes to shut.

What Makes You Burp?

Burrrrrp! What made you do that? You know it's not polite, but you just couldn't help it. Maybe you belched because you ate too fast or drank a lot of soda pop. A burp is your body's way of releasing bubbles of air and other gases from your stomach.

Drinking soda too fast can make you burp.

Facts About Burping

Everyone burps. In fact, most people average about fifteen belches a day. Some burps are loud and noisy. Others are so quiet you may not even notice them. Some foods are more likely than others to make you belch. Examples include onions, peppers, cucumbers, and rich and spicy foods.

Like coughing and sneezing, burping is an involuntary reflex action. When you swallow a lot of air and other gases, the pressure inside your stomach increases. You belch to balance the pressure of gases inside and outside your stomach.

If you drink and eat slowly and chew your food well, you will be less likely to belch. Every burp begins the moment you put food in your mouth. **Salivary glands** in your mouth pour out watery **saliva** to moisten the food. As you chew, your teeth cut up the food and grind it into smaller pieces. Eventually, your tongue forces the food into your esophagus, a tube that leads to your stomach.

Whenever you swallow food, you swallow air along with it. Even saliva is filled with air bubbles. If you are eating in a hurry or if you are trying to talk and eat at the same time, large amounts of air may mix in with your food. If you do not chew the food thoroughly, you may end up swallowing quite a bit of that air.

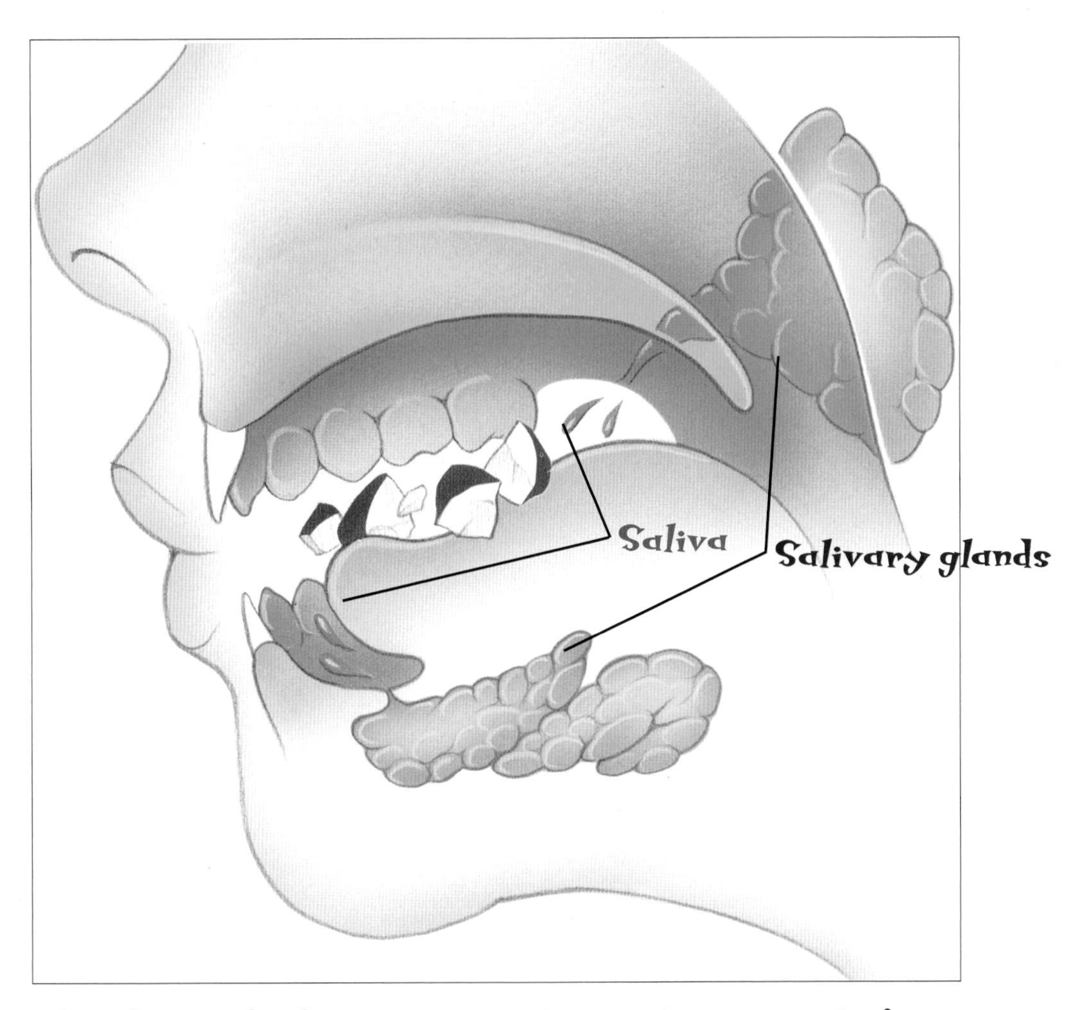

Digestion begins in your mouth. As you chew an apple, it mixes with saliva from your salivary glands.

When food reaches your stomach, it combines with digestive juices and is mixed and churned by strong muscles. If a lot of air has traveled to the stomach along with the food, pressure inside your stomach will build up and your stomach will inflate like a balloon.

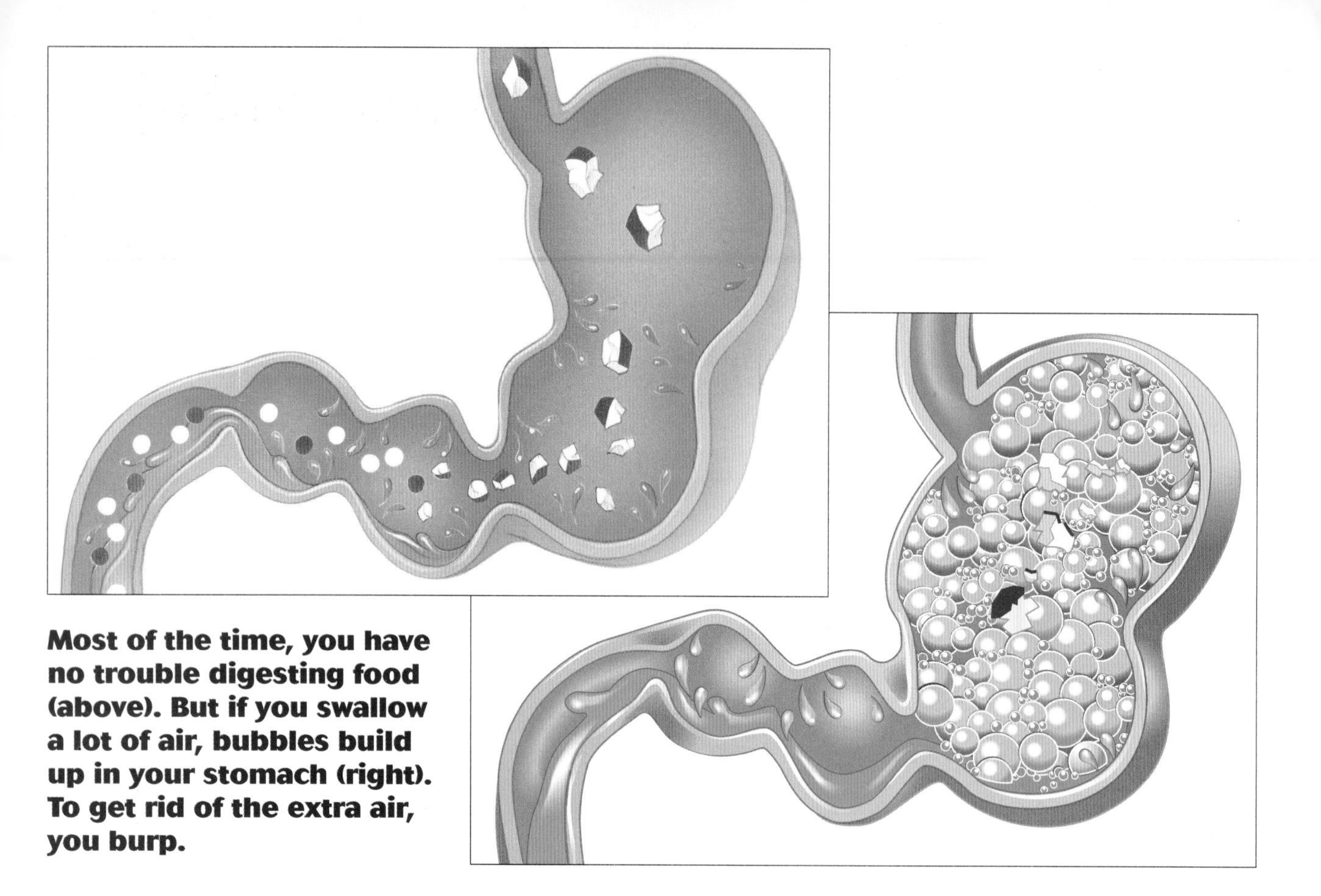

Most of the time, you have no trouble digesting food (above). But if you swallow a lot of air, bubbles build up in your stomach (right). To get rid of the extra air, you burp.

When this happens, the air inside your stomach is pushing outward harder than air outside the stomach is pushing inward. If too much air builds up inside your stomach, some of the gas will whoosh up through your esophagus, and come out of your mouth as a burp.

By the time food leaves the stomach, it has been broken down into tiny particles. These food particles pass into a long, coiled tube called the **small intestine**. The **pancreas** and the **liver** release more digestive juices into the small intestine. Soon, most of the food has turned into a liquid mixture. **Nutrients** in

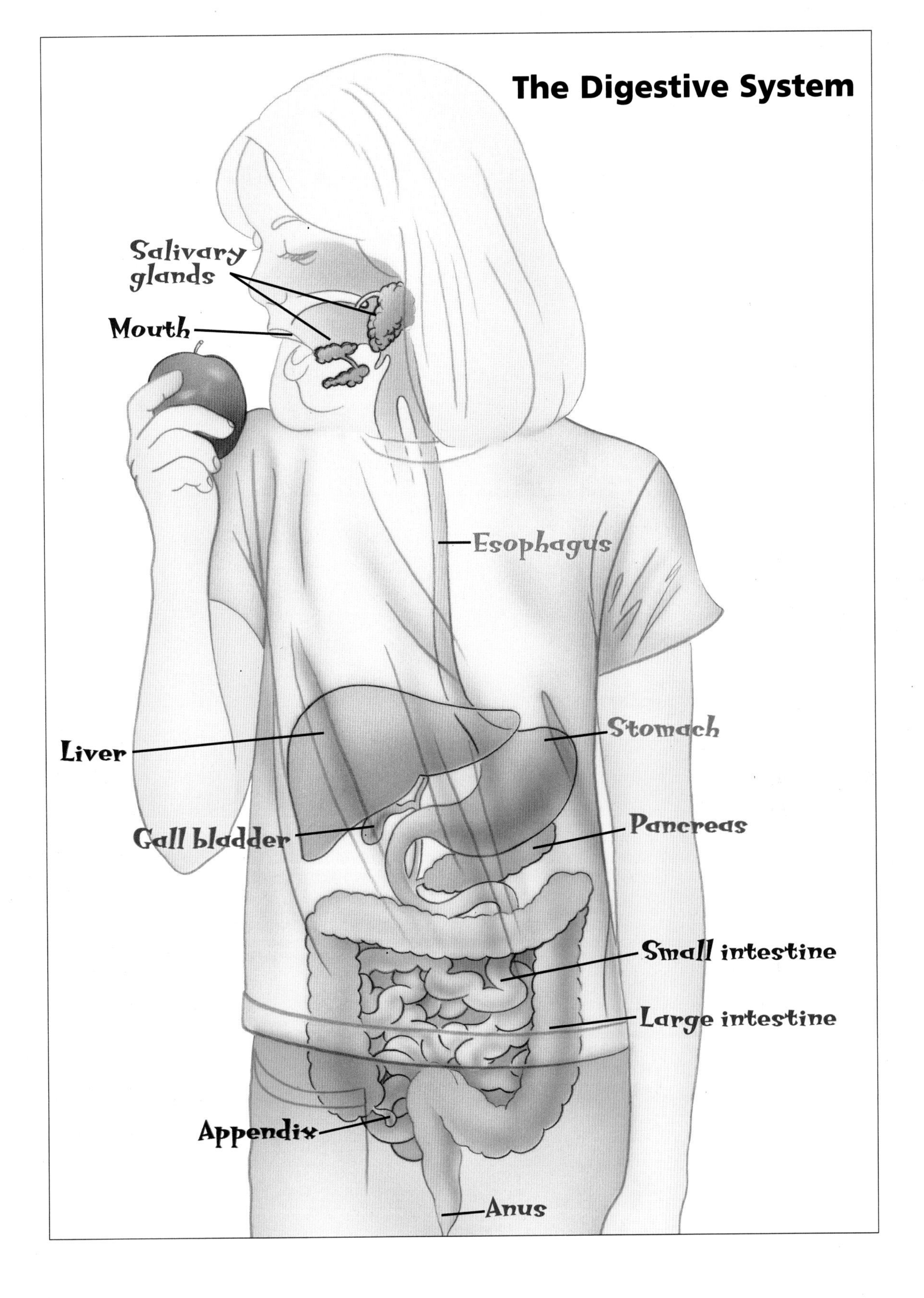
The Digestive System
Salivary glands
Mouth
Esophagus
Liver
Stomach
Gall bladder
Pancreas
Small intestine
Large intestine
Appendix
Anus

the liquid mixture, such as carbohydrates and proteins, pass through the walls of the small intestine and enter your **blood vessels**. As the blood flows through your body, it carries nutrients to all your cells.

Some of the foods you eat cannot be broken into small enough particles to enter your blood vessels. When those larger particles reach the end of the small intestine, they pass into a short, wide tube called the **large intestine**. Extra liquid is then absorbed into the blood, and the undigested food material leaves your body through the anus.

Passing Gas

Radishes, onions, broccoli, and beans are all good sources of fiber.

Fiber—the tough part of vegetables, grains, and fruits—helps to carry away the body's solid wastes. Foods that contain a lot of fiber—such as beans, cabbage, radishes, broccoli, and onions—often cause gas. The gas is produced by **bacteria** that feed on the fiber.

What Makes You Hiccup?

Hic, hic! Oh no! You have the hiccups. You can try to stop them by holding your breath or eating a little sugar, but you may just have to wait patiently until they go away. You can make noises that sound like hiccups, but you cannot make your body hiccup because hiccuping is an involuntary reflex action.

Not only are hiccups annoying, they can also make it difficult to eat, drink, sleep, and talk. The next time you have the hiccups, try one or all of the following remedies. They work for some people!

- Breathe deeply several times.
- Hold your breath.
- Breathe into a paper bag.
- Swallow gulps of water.
- Open your mouth wide and scream.
- Eat a teaspoon of sugar.

Did You Know...

An attack of hiccups usually goes away after a few minutes, but it may last for several hours or, in rare cases, for several days.

Hiccups start in your diaphragm, the large muscle just below your lungs that moves in and out as you breathe.

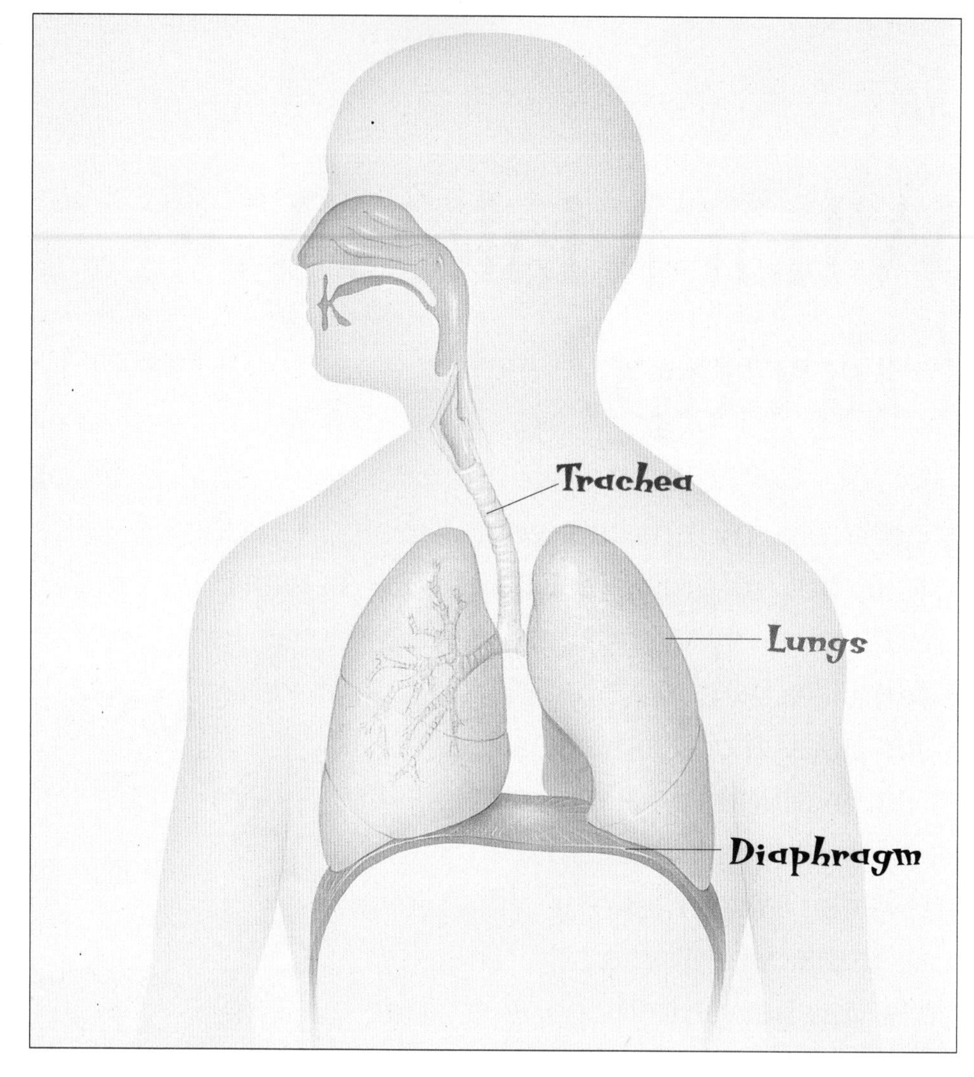

You get the hiccups when your **diaphragm**—the large muscle at the base of your chest that helps you breathe—tightens involuntarily. Most of the time, your diaphragm expands and contracts in a gentle rhythm. But if it suddenly contracts uncontrollably, air rushes into your lungs and your vocal cords snap shut. When the blocked air hits your vocal cords, they make the familiar "hic" sound.

No one knows what causes a person to start hiccuping. Scientists know that some diseases and stomach problems can bring on hiccups. Laughing too hard or getting a fright may also start you hiccuping. To avoid getting the hiccups, try not to eat when you are upset or excited, and do not overeat. You should also drink liquids slowly.

These two friends are having fun laughing. But if they laugh extra hard and long, they may start hiccuping.

What Makes You Yawn?

Yaaaawn! Are you feeling sleepy? Maybe you're just bored, or maybe you are sitting in a stuffy room. Some people yawn when they exercise or sing, but most people yawn when they are relaxed. Yawning is your body's way of getting more **oxygen**.

Why do you think this boy is yawning?

Yawning is one of the many body actions that scientists do not completely understand. Studies have shown that people sometimes yawn even when they are getting plenty of oxygen. Yawning may help your body in other ways too.

When you yawn, you take a very deep breath, which brings oxygen deeper into your lungs. As a result, oxygen enters your blood vessels more quickly than usual. As the blood travels through your body, it delivers the oxygen to your cells. Your cells need oxygen to function.

Here are a few things you can do to avoid yawning.

- Make sure you get plenty of exercise and a good night's sleep.
- If a room is stuffy, open a window or go outside for a while.
- When you have to sit for a long period of time, try moving around in your seat every once in a while.

If you find yourself yawning anyway, try drinking a glass of water or splashing some cold water on your face.

Did You Know...

Have you ever noticed that your eyes feel wet after you yawn? That happens because tiny muscles in your eyelids tighten up when you yawn and a few tears are squeezed out.

This girl is yawning with her mouth wide open.

Some people like to make a lot of noise and even stretch their body when they yawn. Maybe this makes them feel better. However, if you keep your mouth closed when you start to yawn, you won't be a noisy yawner.

Do you think yawning is contagious? Even though yawning is not a disease you can catch, seeing another person yawn may make you want to yawn too. The next time you feel a yawn coming on, ask a friend to watch your face. If you yawn several times, your friend will probably start to yawn too.

When a scientist named Elizabeth Thomas was studying lions in Africa, she was close enough for some of them to see her face. She was surprised to see that when she yawned, one of the lions yawned too. Do you think you could make a pet dog or cat yawn? Try it!

Did you know that lions yawn?

Lions and humans are not the only animals that yawn. You have probably seen a cat or dog yawn. Believe it or not, birds, hippopotamuses, and many other kinds of animals yawn too.

Yawning Manners

You may be able to hide a yawn by forcing your mouth to stay closed, but you can't actually stop a yawn. Like coughing and hiccuping, yawning is an involuntary reflex action. Even if you close your mouth, you will breathe in extra air through your nose. If you have to yawn, place your hand over your mouth. No one wants to see inside your mouth—except your dentist!

What Makes You Blink?

You can't hear a blink, and you usually can't even see one, but blinking is very important. It keeps dust and other particles out of your eyes. It also helps your eyes stay moist.

Every time you blink, your eyelashes brush specks of dust out of your eyes. At the same time, the salty liquid that makes up tears washes particles out of your eyes. The liquid also contains a substance that destroys bacteria.

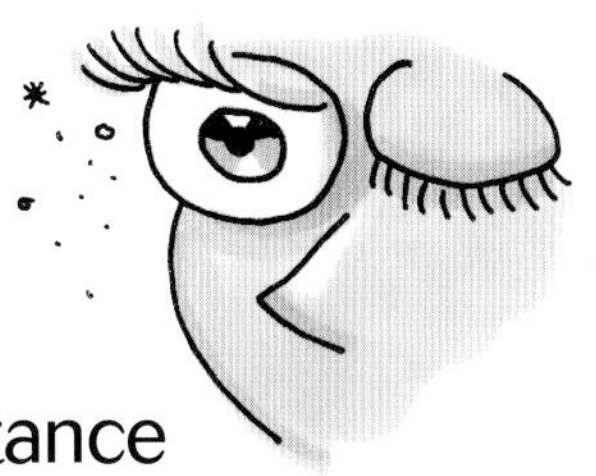

Time for Tears?

A baby's **tear glands** are not fully developed at birth. Newborns may do a lot of crying, but they cannot shed any tears until they are 3 or 4 months old.

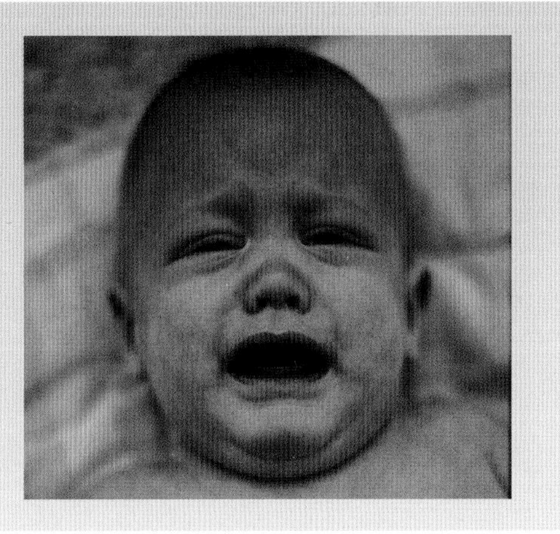

This baby is too young to shed tears.

Activity 2: You Don't Always Think Before You Blink

You can make yourself blink whenever you want to, but you can't stop yourself from blinking. When something suddenly comes close to your face, your blinking reflex automatically closes your eyelids.

Crush a piece of paper into a ball, and have someone toss the ball toward your face. Try not to blink. Were you successful?

Some people blink more often than others do. How long do you think you can go without blinking? To find out, stare into a mirror and start counting slowly until you blink. Ask a friend to do the same thing. Who can go longer without blinking?

Humans are not the only animals that blink. Any animal that has eyelids blinks to keep its eyes clean. A camel's eyes are protected by three sets of eyelids.

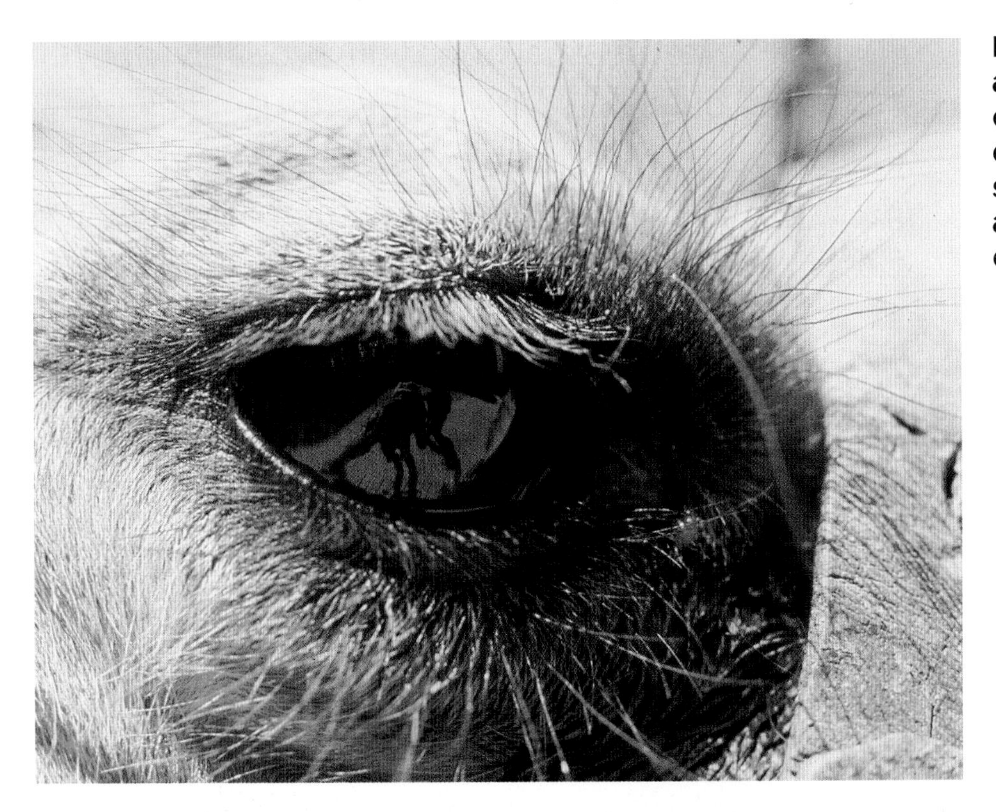

Look carefully at this photo of a camel's eye. Can you see its inner and outer eyelids?

The two outer eyelids have long, curly eyelashes that keep sand from blowing into the camel's eyes. The thin inner eyelids wipe out any dust that gets past the outer eyelids.

Rabbits blink, but they cannot shed tears. Fish don't blink because they have no eyelids. The eyes of a fish are kept moist by the water that flows over them. Birds have three eyelids. The upper and lower eyelids close when a bird is asleep. The third eyelid is the blinking eyelid. It moves sideways.

If you've ever seen a frog, you probably noticed that its eyes bulge out. This helps the animal see in all directions. Frogs shut their eyes by pulling in their eyeballs, which causes their upper and lower eyelids to close. Most frogs also have a third eyelid—a thin,

This bullfrog has three eyelids. One of them is clear, so the frog can see through it when it is closed.

clear inner eyelid attached to the bottom lid. This eyelid can move up over the eye while the frog's eyes are open. This protects the eye without cutting off the frog's vision.

Lack of sleep or rest may cause you to blink a lot. If you think you are blinking too often while reading, watching television, or working at the computer, try to keep your eyes shut for a few moments to give them a little rest. If the problem continues, you should have a doctor check your eyes.

Quick as a Wink

Have you ever quickly closed one eye, but not the other? This is called a wink. Winking is not an automatic reflex because you can control it. Some people can wink either eye, but others can wink only one eye. Can you wink with either eye?

What Makes You Sweat and Shiver?

It's a hot summer day, and you're dripping with sweat. When you sweat so heavily that your clothes get wet, you probably feel uncomfortable. Believe it or not, though, you sweat a little bit all the time.

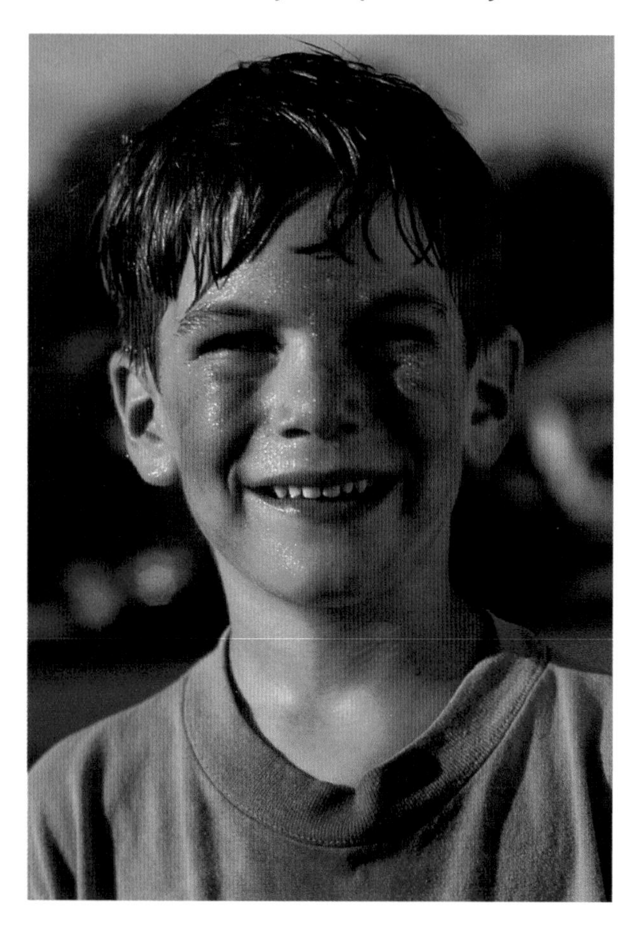

You sweat, or perspire, in cold weather, at night, and even when you are in a swimming pool. When it is cold, the small amount of sweat you produce **evaporates** almost as soon as it forms. Like burping and coughing and blinking, sweating is an involuntary reflex action. You can't control it. It is your body's way of controlling your temperature.

Your body is always sweating, but you produce more sweat on hot days and when you exercise.

This man is wearing a heavy coat, but he still looks cold. Do you think he is shivering?

When you are healthy, your body temperature stays close to 98.6 degrees Fahrenheit (37 degrees Celsius). If your body starts to heat up, you sweat. If your body gets too cold, you shiver. Your skeletal muscles contract and relax rapidly, and sometimes your teeth chatter. Shivering produces extra heat and helps warm your body. Your body will continue to shiver until it returns to its normal temperature.

Shivering is an involuntary reflex action. You can make yourself shiver by standing outside on a cold day, but you can't stop shivering until your body has warmed itself up.

When you get too hot, the **sweat glands** in your skin act as your body's air conditioner. They produce sweat, which is made up of water and a little bit of salt. You have sweat glands all over your body, but especially under your arms, on the palms of your hands, on the soles of your feet, and on your forehead.

A Thirsty Body

When you sweat a lot, your body may become **dehydrated**. That means you are losing more water than you are taking in. Your skin and mucous membranes may feel dry. You should drink more liquids on hot days, when you exercise a lot, or when you have a fever.

The hotter the weather the more you sweat, and the more water your body needs.

Do Other Animals Sweat?

- Dogs have sweat glands, but they can't sweat. To keep cool, a dog lets its tongue hang out of its mouth and breathes quickly. As the dog pants, water evaporates from its mouth and carries away heat.
- Elephants have no sweat glands. They get rid of extra heat by flapping their huge ears or spraying water on themselves with their long trunks.
- A hippopotamus has special glands in its skin that give off a pink, oily liquid. That liquid helps keep the hippo's skin from drying out.

Panting is a dog's way of cooling off.

Why do people often take a shower after exercising? They want to wash off all that extra sweat, but there's also another reason. When sweat first forms on the skin, it has no odor. But as it is broken down by bacteria, it can start to smell really bad. However, sweat glands do not become active until a person is around 10 or 12 years old. As a result, babies and young children do not smell bad when they sweat.

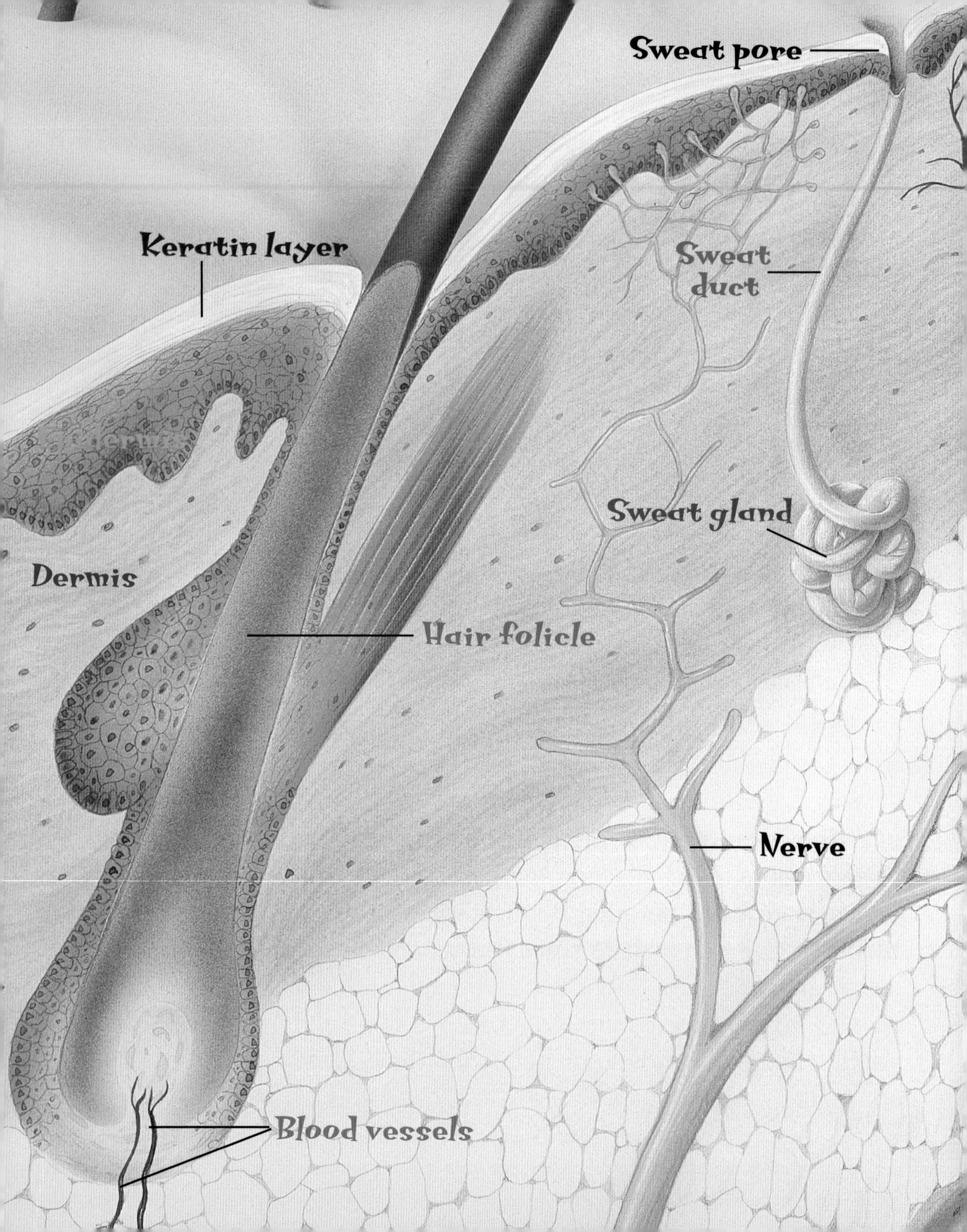
Sweat pore
Keratin layer
Sweat duct
Sweat gland
Dermis
Hair folicle
Nerve
Blood vessels

Sweat glands are located in a layer of skin called the **dermis**. The dermis also contains **hair follicles**, muscles, and nerve endings. The living cells in the dermis are nourished by millions of tiny **blood vessels**.

When sweat leaves the sweat glands, it flows to the surface of the skin through tiny sweat **ducts**. These ducts pass through two more layers of skin cells. The **epidermis**, which also contains living cells, is the middle layer of skin. It is about as thick as a sheet of paper.

When cells in the epidermis die, they move up into the top layer of skin—the **keratin layer**. The dead cells in the keratin layer are squeezed together and flattened to form a thick, tough outer layer that protects your body. The keratin layer keeps germs and other invaders out and keeps moisture in.

This girl has been exercising. As her body heated up, sweat glands in the dermis layer of her skin produced sweat. The sweat passed through the sweat ducts, and left her body through sweat pores in the keratin layer of her skin.

When sweat reaches the top of the keratin layer, it flows out through **pores** and forms tiny drops on the surface of your skin. As the water in sweat evaporates, heat from your body is carried away and you feel cooler. The salt from sweat remains on your skin.

This is what drops of sweat look like through a powerful microscope.

Glossary

bacterium (plural bacteria)—a tiny single-celled organism; some bacteria can cause illness

blood vessel—one of the tubes that carries blood through the body

contagious—a disease that can be spread by contact with someone who is infected with it

dehydrate—to lose water from body tissues

diaphragm—a large muscle between the chest and the stomach

dermis—the inner layer of living skin cells beneath the epidermis. This layer also contains nerves and blood vessels

duct—a tunnel or passageway

epidermis—the outer layer of living skin cells

esophagus—the tube that carries food from the mouth to the stomach

evaporate—to change from a liquid to a gas

fiber—the part of a plant that a person cannot digest

hair follicle—the tube that supports a hair and provides it with nourishment

involuntary reflex action—a muscle action that a person cannot control

keratin layer—the top layer of skin. It is made of a tough protein substance that is also found in hair and nails.

large intestine—the coiled tubelike part of the digestive tract between the small intestine and the anus. It absorbs excess water and prepares undigested food for leaving the body.

liver—a large organ that produces a juice called bile, which helps digest food

mucus—a slimy fluid that coats the inside of the mouth, nose, and throat

mucous membrane—a body tissue that secretes mucus

nerve ending—the tip of a nerve cell. When a nerve ending senses a change, it sends a message to the brain.

nutrient—a chemical in food that is used by the body

oxygen—a gas in the air that your cells need to function

pancreas—an organ that produces digestive juices

pore—the tiny opening of a skin gland

saliva—a watery fluid in your mouth that helps you swallow and digest food

salivary gland—a small organ in the mouth that produces saliva

small intestine—the coiled tubelike part of the digestive tract between the stomach and the large intestine. It breaks down food so that nutrients can be absorbed into blood vessels.

sweat gland—a coiled tube in the skin that produce a watery substance called sweat. Sweat flows to the surface through sweat ducts and passes out of the body through openings called sweat pores.

tear gland—a small organ in the eye that produces tears

trachea—the windpipe; a tube with muscular walls that leads from the throat to the lungs

vaccinate—to give a person a substance that stimulates the body's disease-fighting cells to produce antibodies against a particular kind of germ

voluntary muscle action—a muscle action that a person can control

whooping cough—an infectious coughing disease that occurs in children

Learning More

Books

Catherall, Ed. *Exploring the Human Body*. New Jersey: Raintree Steck-Vaughn, 1992.

Day, Trevor. *1001 Questions and Answers About the Human Body*. New York: Random House, 1994.

Parker, Steve. *Catching a Cold.* New York: Franklin Watts, 1991.

Silverstein, Dr. Alvin, Virginia Silverstein, and Laura Silverstein Nunn. *Common Colds*. Danbury, CT: Franklin Watts, 1999.

Van Cleave, Janice. *The Human Body for Every Kid*. New York: John Wiley, 1995.

Organizations and Online Sites

American Academy of Dermatology
930 Meacham Road
P.O. Box 4014
Schaumburg, IL 60168-4014
http://tray.dermatology.uiowa.edu/

American Academy of Family Physicians
8880 Ward Parkway
Kansas City, MO 64114-2797

Hiccups
http://onhealth.com/ch1/resource/conditions/item,366.asp
To find out more about hiccups, check out this Web page.

KidsHealth.org
http://www.kidshealth.org
This site has loads of information on infections, behavior and emotions, food and fitness, and growing up healthy. It also has health games and animations. A search option lets you search for "yawn" or "sweat" or other health conditions. The site was created and is maintained by medical experts at The Nemours Foundation.

Why Do I Have Gas?
http://www.onhealth.com/ch1/resource/othersources/item,44482.asp
The information on this Web page was provided by the National Institute of Diabetes and and Digestive and Kidney Diseases. It has all kinds of information about burping and passing gas and describes ways to avoid and treat these conditions.

The Yuckiest Site on the Internet: Your Gross and Cool Body—Skin
http://www.nj.com/yucky/body/systems/skin/
This site has all kinds of fun information about human skin.

Index

About the Author

Jean Stangl is a former elementary classroom teacher and an early childhood specialist. She has taught early childhood classes at the community college and university levels. She has also taught summer science-enrichment programs for children in grades 3–6 as well as writing classes and workshops for adults. She is a regular speaker at educational conferences, and her book, *How to Get Your Teaching Ideas Published*, has been used as a college textbook.

In the last 15 years, Ms. Stangl has written more than 30 books and 250 magazine articles for children and teachers. She is a member of the California Reading Association, the Society of Children's Book Writers and Illustrators, and the Southern California Council on Literature for Children and Young People.

Ms. Stangl lives in Camarillo, California, with her husband. She enjoys traveling, swimming, gardening, collecting old children's books, and spending time with her children and grandchildren.